Woodland Fauna

LEVEL 5

/oe/au/

Teaching Tips

Green Level 5

This book focuses on the phonemes **/oe/au/**.

Before Reading

- Discuss the title. Ask readers what they think the book will be about. Have them briefly explain why.
- Ask readers to sort the words on page 3. Read the sounds and words together.

Read the Book

- Encourage readers to break down unfamiliar words into units of sound. Then, ask them to string the sounds together to create the words.
- Urge readers to point out when the focused phonics phonemes appear in the text.

After Reading

- Encourage children to reread the book independently or with a friend.
- Ask readers to name other words with /oe/ or /au/ phonemes. On a separate sheet of paper, have them write the words out.

Library of Congress Cataloging-in-Publication Data is available at www.loc.gov or upon request from the publisher.

ISBN: 979-8-88996-849-8 (hardcover)
ISBN: 979-8-88996-850-4 (paperback)
ISBN: 979-8-88996-851-1 (ebook)

Photo Credits

Images are courtesy of Shutterstock.com. With thanks to Getty Images, Thinkstock Photo and iStockphoto. Cover – Eric Isselee. 4–5 – Blaj Gabriel, Lea Cabrera. 6–7 – Pressmaster, WildMedia. 8–9 – Szymon Bartosz, WildMedia. 10–11 – Erik Mandre, Menno Schaefer, Vaclav Sebek. 12–13 – Hero Images, PepeQuilez. 14–15 – Purino, Steve Simkins. 16 – Shutterstock.

Can you sort all the words on this page into two groups?

Foe

Aloe

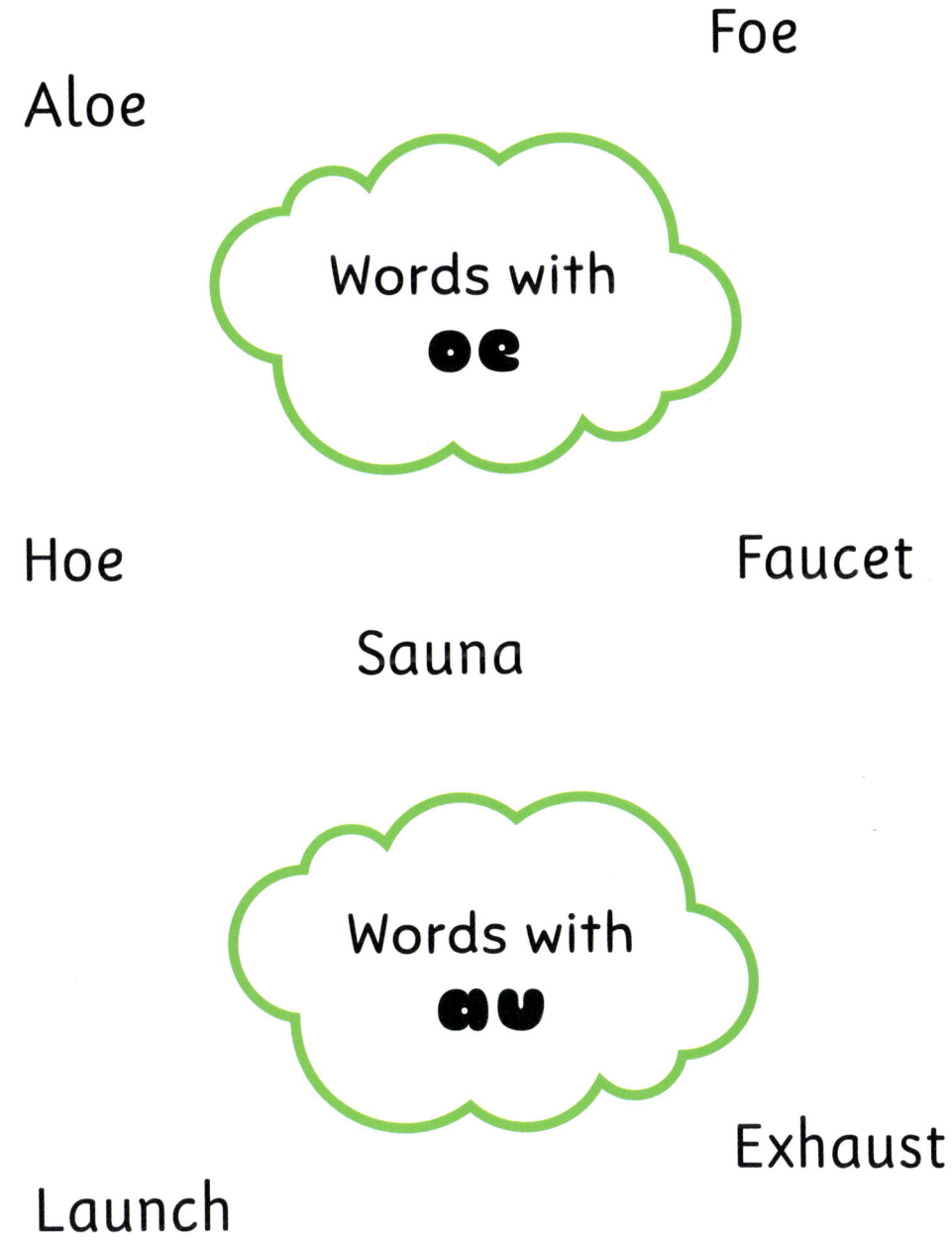

Words with
oe

Hoe

Faucet

Sauna

Words with
au

Exhaust

Launch

Have you ever been to the woods? If you have, you might have seen some woodland fauna. Fauna means animals.

Woods

You might spot some animals if you tiptoe in and keep still. Do not stomp or you will spook them.

Stay alert. Can you hear or see an animal near you? It might be on the lookout for food.

If you see a big animal saunter past,
it could be a doe or a buck.

Buck

Doe

If it has antlers, it might be a buck. If there are no antlers, it might be a doe.

Antlers

Bucks shed their antlers, but they come back as the year goes on. The antlers will come back bigger than they were when they fell off.

If you see a flash of auburn as a little animal goes past, it could be lots of different things.

It could be a fox or a squirrel. Each has a tail with lots of fur on it.

Squirrel

Fox

If you cannot see an animal near you, you can check for tracks.

Different woodland animals have different feet. You can tell what an animal is from just one track!

If you see a track from a long, cleft hoof, it might be from a buck or doe.

Cleft hoof

If you see a track with little toes, it might be from a fox, skunk, raccoon, or you!

Sound out each word. Does it have an /oe/ or /au/ sound?

oboe  laundry

tomatoes

sauce